For my family, and yours.

WHEN WE SAY
BLACK
LIVES
MATTER

MAXINE BENEBA CLARKE

wren
&rook

Little one,

when we say
Black Lives Matter,

we're saying Black people are wonderful-strong.

That we deserve to be
treated with basic RESPECT,
and that history's done us wrong.

Little love, when we call out
Black Lives Matter,
we're saying *walk with us*,
r*aise* your voice:

When we scream out Black Lives Matter,
and we march, against falling night,
we're saying enough is **enough** is **enough**,
and we need to put things right.

Darling, when we sing that Black Lives Matter, and we're dancing through the streets,

we're saying: fear will not destroy our joy, defiance in our feet.

When we *w i s p e r*
Black Lives Matter,
we're remembering
the past.

All the terrible things
that were said and done,

we're saying they
trouble our hearts.

When
we
sob
that
Black Lives Matter,

we're saying trouble
still **STALKS**,
to this day:

that we've seen it
monster in the shadows,

and must all help **drive** *it* away.

My sweet, when we **bellow**
Black Lives Matter, we're saying:
ain't no freedom, till we get ours.

And *all* Black folk still suffering,
we'll **STAND** with you, we *vow*.

When we **smile**
Black Lives Matter,
we're raising our spirits high.

We're saying:
we are here,
and we are **enough**.

Black-beautiful-brave,
my child.

When we **laugh** that Black Lives Matter, that's the ancestors, inside:

a-thundering on djembe drums
and guiding us, steady, to rise.

When we *know* that
Black Lives Matter,
then darling, we know our worth:

that we are as **precious**
as every soul

whose story has
journeyed the Earth.

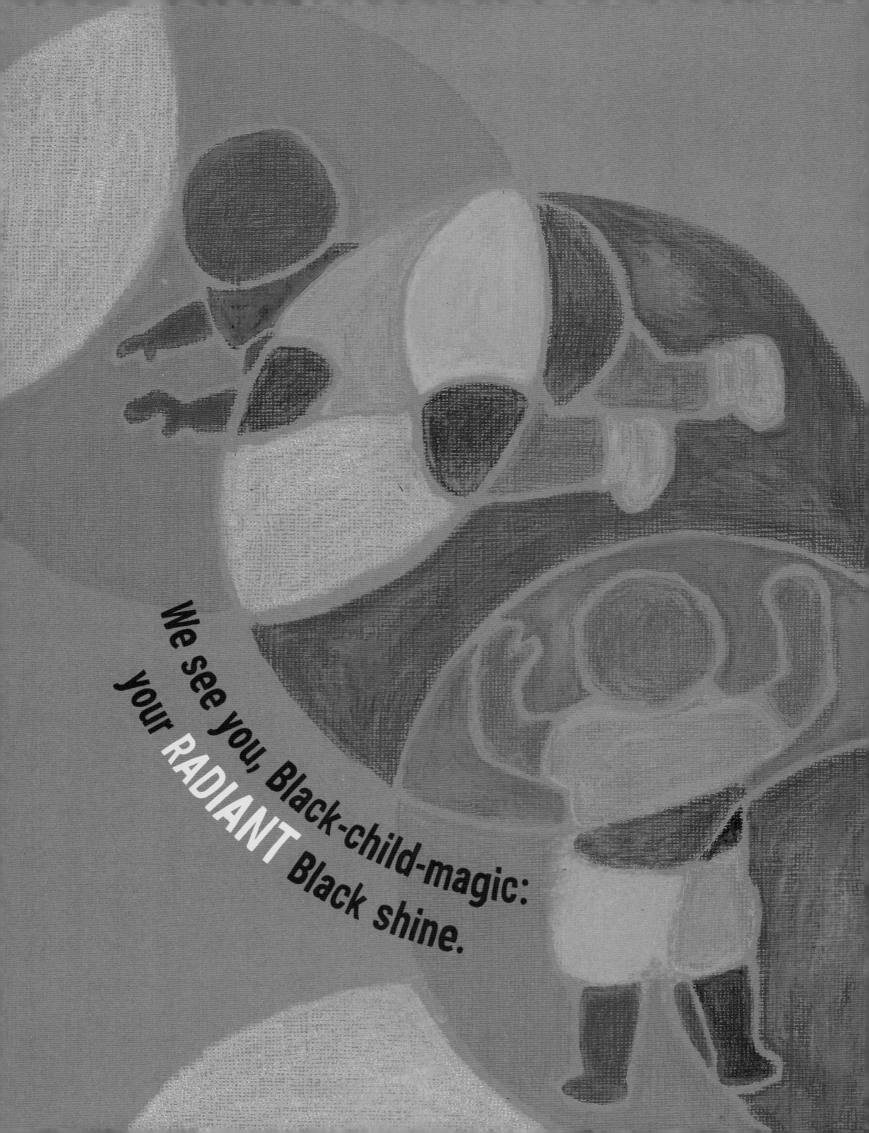

We see you, Black-child-magic: your RADIANT Black shine.

and we **KNOW** we'll be alright.

First published in Great Britain in 2021 by Wren & Rook

First published in Australia and New Zealand in 2020 by Lothian Children's Books, Hachette Australia

HB ISBN: 978 1 5263 6397 8
PB ISBN: 978 1 5263 6398 5
E-book ISBN: 978 1 5263 6399 2

10 9 8 7 6 5 4 3 2 1

Wren & Rook
An imprint of
Hachette Children's Group
Part of Hodder & Stoughton
Carmelite House
50 Victoria Embankment
London EC4Y 0DZ

An Hachette UK Company
www.hachette.co.uk
www.hachettechildrens.co.uk

Publishing Director: Debbie Foy
Art Director: Laura Hambleton

Internal design by Kinart

Printed in China